Did You Find Everything You Were Looking For?

Did You Find Everything You Were Looking For?

POEMS

Donna Masini

W. W. NORTON & COMPANY

Independent Publishers Since 1923

In memory of my parents

To Mallory, Ryan, and Jacob Kusterer

On tragic mountain passes
the wind rips hats from unwitting heads
and we can't help
laughing at that.

—Wisława Szymborska

Reconcile yourself to wait in the darkness . . .
—*The Cloud of Unknowing*

. . . but time and chance happen to them all.
—Ecclesiastes

Contents

Did You Find Everything You Were Looking For?

Meditation

The man on the screen is talking about monkey mind.
A metaphor, he says, from India, a country "teeming
with monkeys." Ubiquitous, erratic, leaping through trees,

hotel rooms. The only monkeys she's seen were caged.
Aren't monkeys notoriously promiscuous?
Lip-smacking, intractable, they chatter,

manacled in her mind. Humans,
he says, experience three thoughts per second.
Seconds tick by.

You just had thirty thoughts, he says.
But she'd had only one: How long has it been?
How long since she's been touched?

He's going to teach her how to have a quiet mind.
What beautiful legs he has. What skin.
Why wouldn't he have a quiet mind,

a man with skin like this? She's been ticking with desire,
the whole restless island ticking, thrumming. Crickets, bees,
the insistent incessant wind, the shimmer and buzz.

Imagine your mind an ocean, the man says. She lies back.
He touches her stomach, her hip. No, it is her mind
touching her, her mind with his hands. Her mind

tugs the edge of her . . . slips its fingers into
her mind has a mind of its own.
If only it were someone else's.

I mind how once we lay. Had she substituted writing
for sex? *and plunged your tongue to my . . .*
She'd watched two sparrows mate that morning.

Three seconds. Was that desire?
Do gorillas feel desire, she once asked a man. Ask a gorilla,
he said. I just did, she said. They were at Film Forum.

She lay there yesterday—half an hour, oxytocin juicing
through her. It felt good but did it count as meditation?
Why is she always counting?

She was meditating so she'd have something to write
in her notebook, but after, it was still just monkeys
jumping, climbing the limbic system, coiling and spooning in her

mind. Or was that her brain? The amygdala nestled in the . . .
Is desire an emotion? Can you long yourself to death?
Surrender, the man is saying, let your thoughts come.

This is definitely not meditation.
His voice, her mind. The monkeys
clanking their chains, rattling their manacles.

1

Is There Anything Else I Can Help You With?

Can you help me find a medication for my mother's dementia and dress shoes that don't hurt my feet?

Will you go to Trader Joe's and pick up the red onions I forgot and remind me to bring my cloth bag next time?

Can you tell me why so much of the plastic we recycle is dumped into landfills?

I would like to understand how a credit-card-sized mosaic of microplastic ends up in our bodies every day—is this true?—and why I spent half an hour this morning playing a 37-second clip of Sylvia Plath laughing.

Is there a word for when you're leaning over the stove waiting for coffee and the previous night's dream keeps almost appearing?

Can we say things happened that only happened in our minds? I've had dreams that feel more real than vast stretches of seventh grade. And who's to say, given the many times I've read *To the Lighthouse*, Mrs. Ramsay is any less real than my cousin Aldo?

Is there a name for what you feel when you look into a store window and don't recognize yourself?

And why do the tears you shed in emotion—like when your mother gropes for a word you know is daughter and wants to know if she is dead— contain 20–25% more protein than those you shed chopping onions?

A Vietnamese monk told his audience in Vermont that if they were very very mindful with each bite, they would be present not only in that moment, which was decades ago, but would, in fact, experience the tomato they were eating back to the dirt, the vine, the sun as it poured into it, back inside the moment of its creation.

Is there a word for that?

What would I have to chew to be able to laugh on the phone with my sister again?

Can you help me with that?

Notebook

This morning I woke up hearing a voice saying *the urn is half full.*

—

In Orange, Connecticut, near the house in which Josef Albers lived, was a green sign with white letters that said, "This is Orange."

—

"At the time I searched desperately inside myself for some memory of happiness. Now I learn I was part of someone else's happiness."

Whose happiness have I been a part of?

To the Woman in Window 8 at the DMV

I'm sorry I didn't have what you called the original copy of my birth certificate. I did bring my official infant footprints. They're nothing like my feet now, but it did say Certificate of Birth. Yes, it was a Xerox.

Tell me, how can an original be a copy?

Maybe you had a disappointing lunch. Couldn't find a parking spot. Don't even drive. I don't drive. You could see that from my expired learner's permit. I was only asking for a REAL ID.

What is real, Window 8? It seems to me nothing could be more real than my 2¾-inch infant foot.

I'm terrified of dying. *Driving.*

I'm sorry that, paying you for the useless-for-federal-purposes-non-driving ID, I saw you type in the wrong birthdate. I wasn't born in 1931. You did ask me to check for accuracy. My father was born in 1931. If he hadn't died four years ago, he might have made you laugh. But maybe he'd have been just another old guy at your window waiting to die.

A few years before he died, my father had to stop driving. That was terrible.

There were many terrible things in my life, Montaigne says, *and most of them never happened.*

I would like to read more Montaigne.

When your father dies, I hope you'll be with him, peering into his fogging oxygen mask. I held my father's arm, thanked him for everything I hadn't thanked him for as I stomped around in my glowering adolescence.

Have you tried meditation? Smoldering rage isn't good for our hearts. It's a heartbreaking world. Entropy. Dirty Money. They are bombing hospitals. Maybe you were imagining the Sixth Extinction. Even one is terrible.

Have a baby anyway. I wish I had. With the right mix of genes and circumstance you could've been my daughter.

Listen, someday what will be left of us—a few teeth, pitted bones—

Did you even look at my footprint? Miraculous, isn't it? I wonder why prehistoric walls aren't covered with baby footprints. Have you seen those caves? Like giant hand-covered wombs.

That woman in your head—there are ways to stop her. Anger can mask grief. So much to be angry about: proliferating viruses, economy seating. Screw the DMV, Window 8.

I wish your window had a lake view, and cardinals singing their unmistakable *cheer*. A window needn't be a cage.

The phone numbers of my dead are floating up inside me.

I'm not sure I agree with Montaigne. Terrible things are real even if they happen only in our minds.

I wish the birth of anything were so miraculous no one could ever bomb a hospital. I wish I'd been nicer, sooner, to my father.

Suffering is a choice. If your feet hurt as you walk, the Buddhists say, think about the absence of pain in the foot that lifts. Focus on relief, you'll feel relief.

We suffer so much, trapped in our windows, thinking we're looking through them.

I'll never see you again, Window 8. My dead friends? I'll never dial their numbers again.

Two weeks from now, when my useless non—REAL ID arrives in my mailbox, I'll think of you and I will remain, always, ticket 4180

On Time

(a 2½-minute read)

Tomorrow, my grandfather would say when I asked
him to ride my bike. Next day, I'd ask again: You said
you'd ride my bike today. No, he'd say, I said tomorrow.

This would go on for days. In Italian the idea of the future
is contained in the present: I ride your bike is the same as I will ride
your bike tomorrow and I am riding your bike right now.

What a slippery world. *Che sarà, sarà!*
Each time my mother reaches for a word—toothpaste, candle—
each time I forget a noun, I see that rickety old train of thought,

late again, sluggish, chugging around its ________.
Nouns are the first to go, the doctor says to the grandmother
in the sad Korean movie whose title, I remember, is *Poetry.* And the last?

When did articles start saying things like "a 6-minute read"?
You have 140 minutes left of this book, it says on my iPad screen.
And if I put the iBook down, for, say, two weeks?

That's a way to stretch a minute! This is the 20th century,
my mother exclaimed the other night. Time is running out
to save the Western Bumblebee I learn today at 10:49.

A short text. A 30-second plea. I'm asked to rush my 27 dollars.
Immediately. I'm late. Here at my desk how is it possible
I'm also looking up into the window of my father's hospital room,

four years ago, watching him wave. He's just taught me to play solitaire.
How is it possible I've seen only one sunrise in my life?
Did you know that memory has the same root as mourn?

An ounce of cocaine, the painter says, costs about sixty times more
than an ounce of oil paint, but lasts only an hour, while cadmium red
lasts hundreds of years. Well, time is money, as my grandfather,

who had neither, would say. Out of joint. Looping around.
How can you finish knitting an infinity scarf?
Row row row, merrily merrily merrily, row merrily row.

A vicious cycle. A brief candle. Tomorrow and tomorrow and tomorrow.
You have 140 minutes left.
Why do we say someone who's dead is late?

Diorama

Look at me, hung with priceless objects,
endlessly revisiting my museum of stuff, rotating
exhibits loaned by donors. My mother's eyelashes

catch in her hat veil. I am young. It was the future
that looked luminous. So much of it. Here now
her lacey mind—her brain's cruel erasures.

What a homeless gaggle of nomads, her thoughts
floating in their foamy sodas,
giddy insomniacs opening their throats.

A dusty silence stares out of
the long shelf-life memory of doll.
Look at me. What is this mania for saving?

Whoever said you can't fix the past
never made a diorama. But what to do
with all these teeth and clip-on earrings.

The baker, the tin angel, the tiny French horn
that hung from my grandmother's tree.
Give me the land of motionless childhood,

my sister's plastic curler.
Every book feels like a library book.
Every spoon a loan. Why love it all so intensely?

Window of minutes, window of turning back
clocks. Cold backseat window with splattering rain.
O, box of me rattling. Here is a collage called father.

Here is my mother's hairbrush.

Beauty Parlor, 1970

Propelled by an idea of elegance, I asked
for Grecian curls. What had gotten into my head?
I never looked more unlike myself.
A face attached to a concoction
of locks. More construction than girl, Aqua Net
confabulation. Reflections of women
nod and drift under hoods, like
astronauts through magazines. *Life. Look.*
Pink curlers nestle like baby pigs.
Beauticians line up in turquoise smocks,
silver clips clipped to their pockets.
I'd wanted tendrils. But were these tendrils
snaking my face like . . . *Like?*
Like like like. Everything was like something,
reminded me of—what? Whose
open-mouthed yowl was that in the mirror?

She was a shield, a model of painted rage,
head bobbing in the aqua mists
of someone else's conflagration,
rhinestone tiara pinned to her hair.
What did she know of beauty?
Her face launched no ship. She dreamed
she went to Vietnam in her Maidenform Bra.
Nose in a book she bashed herself into mythic windows,
their curtain-parting apocalypses. A legendary head,
an epic neck, an hourglass of disaster inside her:

napalm, the burning girl, the paper boy dead.
Life. Look. Is that a propeller on her head?
She is not the first to love and despise the likes of Achilles.
Poor stupid raging boy coming at her with his war
cry to slaughter her with her own mirror.

Prayers

Her mind wanders, full of what
she calls "detritus." She wonders
whether anyone uses the nylon sheath
that comes with a new umbrella, and how
rarely she turns the correct burner knob
on the first try, and why, if 9 took ages
to spin on a rotary phone, we dialed 911
in an emergency. She thinks
she should be thinking about important things,
like all these wildfires, but what can she do
about wildfires except watch the smoldering
satellite views on the *Times* homepage, repeating
gusts of smoke spewing from the core, watching
disaster turn abstract—its play of pinks, reds, grays,
these wind-driven fronts of flame, collapse, updraft,
spinning vortices of fire and air pumping heat—
miles acres heights, speed trees lives—she can't fathom
the numbers. How helpless her mind is. Still,
when she hears a siren, she says a quick prayer—
a habit of childhood—opens, over the suffering,
her flimsy precarious parasol of thought.

Kyoto 1

Even in Kyoto / I yearn for Kyoto / and the cuckoo's call.　—Bashō

I've never been to Kyoto, but I've stood by a lake in the Adirondacks so afraid I'd forget the blue call of the loon that I dropped my phone in the water as I tried to record it.

I am rarely where I am.

When I'm looking at a painting I'm often distracted, worried I'll miss the train or there won't be a postcard.

◆

I understand being in a place and wanting
to be there. Like marriage.
I was there and longing for it
at the same time. Though perhaps I wasn't
longing for that marriage, in that moment.
Not until it ended.

◆

Was Bashō married?
Is it Bashō or Issa—the flies wringing their hands, wringing their feet?
They look the same: seventeen syllables. 5–7–5.

I would love a stranger, right now, to whisper seventeen syllables
　　in my ear.

Midnight in the Pain Relief Aisle of CVS Thinking about *The Cloud of Unknowing*

Pain ricochets around my skull
like an aspirin commercial from the '60s,
darting up the nasal passages, up behind the frown,

the temporal bones, clutching at God
like a desperate spark. *He bound you to him
by a chain of such longing.* Ridiculous

this pressing and pressing the button for an attendant,
aching jaw, temples throbbing. When did they start
locking everything up? Do I need something,

this man wants to know. Contact lens solution,
root touch-up. Where is my mind?
my mother said this morning. Is Daddy dead?

How did he die? *Do not fret after God,* my book says.
Well, I do fret. I'm fretted as a guitar, picking out
the same chords, arpeggios of dread wandering 24-hour chains,

rehearsing my facts, one big cloud of forgetting.
There are 300 muscles in the face. The time bone, the temple
is called, where our hair grays first. Why aren't the aisles marked?

My God, what is that shrieking? The man doesn't work here,
he says. *Reconcile yourself to wait in the darkness.*
What did I think spiritual desert meant? Surely not that

lump of nothing I was an hour ago on the couch, wielding
the remote, spooning mango sorbet out of a container.
It should feel, I explain to the self-checkout screen

(how did I get here?), punching in my customer number,
more important. What saints felt. A dreadful hunger.
If you need help, the self-checkout voice is saying.

Todo y nada, todo y nada it whispers
here in the aching all-night fluorescent.

Did You Find Everything You Were Looking For

the young man at the supermarket register says. She'd found this piece of raw salmon in its plastic package. An onion. Milk. But was that the right word? Doesn't to find a thing suggest it's been lost? She's trying to stop revisiting her history of losses. The heart-shaped ring her godmother gave her on Communion Day which she'd lost in the snow on the way home from Girl Scouts. Her godmother, who'd recently died. Her cats. *Four* cats. So many things she's never found. She never found what had caused the leak in the ceiling that ruined her grandfather's prayerbook. What made the tumor grow in her sister's lung. She hadn't found the great love of her life. Well, she had found him. She'd divorced him. In truth she's never understood what great love of your life means exactly, but she'd found, that morning, great solace when she looked up from her book to see her cat (she'd found that cat after the last two died) gazing at her with what she felt pretty sure was love, when it slipped its delicate paw into her hand. One night that cat snatched the salmon poaching in the pan. She found the word *poaching*, with regard to the cat and the salmon, funny. She likes to laugh. She finds it helps to laugh. It's a mystery to her that she finds herself alive on a particular day, after so many years— picking up milk, waiting on lines. How quickly it all passes, then you find yourself standing among the late-night shoppers, the piled-up carts and baskets, the winter dark pressing against the store windows, and this beautiful young man wanting to know.

Dust

What made me think of him—the man who, years ago, confessed
how, night after night, he cruised the streets in his mother's duster,
lusting for a pickup, the way I imagined the dull cotton

half-buttoned housecoat floating behind him
even after he explained that the Duster was a car.
I still see that dust-colored shift,

the breezy material of his longing seeking release
behind every shrub. I'd been watching the kettle steam,
half-listening to the news, listing words like *seed* or *cleave*

that mean a thing and its opposite. To dust is to brush off, wipe clean,
unless you're talking crops or cake pans. I was afraid of it. The way it
floated across our living room. The first dust I touched surprised me.

The grit in the fluff. Fuzz skin lint dander. Where did it come from?
Disgusting, my mother said, slippers slapping across the living room,
balled up tissue in the ambiguous pockets of her duster. Don't touch it.

I love the promiscuous slips and shifts over time, the way
those slippers were called *thongs* but are now *flip-flops*,
thongs being quite another thing. I love the shifts of mind—

The Steam of Consciousness, a student called it.
I explained her mistake, but soon began to see the steam
rising, picking up dust, dust seeding clouds, rain falling

on crops, pooling, steaming up, consciousness assuming, wave on
steamy wave, its various forms—memory thought perception—
and you can't say why the puddle becomes your mother.

Why, this morning, watching the kettle steam,
did I think of that man, the way my mistake made him laugh,
seemed to pick him up, help him imagine

what was driving him, all those nights—fear, perhaps,
where our mistakes might lead us, the dust we've been
and would become. And why, now, remember my dead

sister's joke, that, briefly, years ago, settled
my fear: *Look under my bed, mom,*
'cause someone's either coming or going.

Postcard

Though it looks like a dusty flat-screen TV
I want you to see the way this Venetian sky
effaces the famous 150 canals and fades
into morning. Yesterday I left St. Mark's to shop,
escape the anxious mosaic epitaphs, the crazed saints
climbing the walls. There's always tomorrow.
I'd love to walk with you tomorrow, but I'll be hunting,
an old man said last week. The kind of random anecdote
I save for you. Were you not dead, you'd laugh.
Venice is still dying. Shiny. Nothing to buy.
I wish I were here.

2

Notebook

I've been practicing impermanence again, seeing everyone as a corpse.
Corpses walking down Houston St., staring into cell phones with haircuts
and rain boots, waiting for the light to change.

My book says to contemplate the decomposition of my body, the Nine
Stages of Decay: bloating, putrefaction, rotting flesh, worms, bone, etc. To
meditate on this until I'm calm, at peace, a smile on my face.

Where will it be, my body? Infinity Burial Suit? Egg-shaped death pod?
Traditional coffin?

My body lies over the ocean   oh bring back my body to me

The cardiologist asked if I'd ever seen a cardiologist before. Only socially,
I said. Were we flirting? Was there something wrong with my heart?
I asked. Why would you think that? he said. Well, why was I there?

Then I was lying on the exam table, the radiologist smearing me with cold
gel. She looked into my heart, clicking, snapping pictures. On her screen,
waves going *swish swish swish*. My heart looked like a baby. A fish mouth
opening, closing, saying *lonely lonely lonely*. Or *holy holy holy*.

She moved her wand among the various chambers. No one's ever looked so closely at my heart.

Hard to concentrate on what I'm writing. I keep noticing how my handwriting's changed. When did this happen?

When you Google something, suggestions pop up while you're typing. Often the grammar's wrong, as if the person is too anxious to do anything but plug in a few words.

"This sample handwriting from a spry, healthy ninety-seven-year-old shows good control, balance, a disciplined but flowing style that combines angles and curves. A brain that has worked well for almost a century."

"The talk, in which Ms. Lee wore the death suit and discussed 'training' mushrooms to eat her own nail clippings, skin and hair, has been viewed by more than 1.3 million people."

Find the Infinity Burial Suit notes you took last year.

"The Hotel Relation is what Japanese call an 'itai hoteru,' or corpse hotel. Rooms are fitted with small altars and narrow platforms designed to hold coffins. Checkout time, for the living and the dead, is usually no later than 3 p.m."

"What is the inside of a pillow called?"

If your handwriting looks like this, it can be an early sign of Parkinson's, dementia, Alzheimer's, essential tremor . . .

"Lift up your heart to God with humble love and mean God himself, and not what you want from him."   Meister Eckhart??

One need not be a Chamber to be haunted.

In the café they were playing "I Left My Heart in San Francisco." Where is Tony Bennett's heart now?

Is my handwriting more legible with this pen Catherine gave me? I think it is. Buy another one later. Try it for a week.

Later they sent the images of my heart, but I couldn't open the portal.

My Father Teaches Me to Play Solitaire

by the window of his hospital room. So late in the day
and he won't let us cheat. Cards slipping on his rickety tray,

the orderly rows collapsing into one another,
his hand diminishing, he turns over the one card

that won't fit anywhere. We couldn't finish.
Wait, I said, we're almost done. He shook his head.

Luck, chance. No skill involved. No will. No bluff. No time
to start a new game. I left my father waving in his window.

Days later I bought a deck, shuffled the stiff cards, set them up
the way he'd shown me, and—beginner's luck?—I won.

Can you win a game you've played alone? No need to display
a poker face to yourself. No kidding, he said, I just won too.

My father's a joker. Bruno, our neighbor used to say,
you're a card. So no surprise what he taught me:

when you're done you have nothing in your hand.

Mouthguard to Kierkegaard

Wielding his prong pliers and steel pick, with his tiny
dime-sized mirror and blinding headlamp, he peers into the crumbling

roots. Excavator, he says, tightening the metal clamp and rubber dam,
my teeth crooked as stones in a country graveyard. Erosion, he says.

Sometimes I think it's loneliness syphoning the calcium
from my teeth and bones. Bone cold loneliness, like a greedy fetus.

Lose a tooth for every child, they used to say. Turns out it's true.
I've heard that birds eat the shells of their hatched eggs. Smart birds.

I never had a child. Big gap there, he says, his scaler poking. I have a box
of baby teeth my mother saved (four kids, all that's left of one of them)

and the first tooth I lost. The note my mother wrote the tooth fairy.
She was a brave girl, my mother told the fairy. My mother

has few teeth left and lives in a unit called The Bridges.
I will show you fear in a handful of teeth. Is this hurting you,

the dentist says. I open my eyes. Are you feeling pain?
he says, headlamp glaring as if he's investigating a crime.

I'm imagining, I say—drain nozzle jiggling, water streaming
down my chin—what it would feel like without . . . I reach from under

my disposable gown, point to the jawful of Novocain.
Why would you do that, he wants to know. As if it were a choice.

What have I ever *really* chosen? Why haven't I taken better care?
Teeth should last a lifetime. How long is that?

I'm numb. Decaying. What will I do with this mouthful of neglect?
You grind, he says. You need a guard.

The Memory House

My mother wants to go home. She's worried about the farm. *What farm?* In the country of compassionate deception I must not challenge her. Do you see chickens or pigs? is not helpful. Lovely, I say, pointing to the couch, and which is your favorite pig?

◆

The mind unminded. The MRI lighting up, narrowing corridors, the brain's mischievous trampoline, and what was one glitch is now a mother.

Suddenly her life's a *trompe l'oeil.* She floats outside her capsule of habit in a room of strangers slumped over Hangman.

The word is cellophane. Comforting old word. See-through sheet across a breathing diorama. Lights dim as day advances, then twinkle to simulate a starry sky.

Life becomes lighting. Trick of the eye? A lie? *Who knows I'm here?* Where? *Somewhere.*

◆

Some days she's all adverb. Not who or what, but how? How much? How often? Where? Now somewhere is a gap in the channel. An aisle of silence. She clutches the remote. Someone has given her a doll.

◆

anxiously sadly painfully suspiciously nervously mindlessly

◆

The more she forgets, the more I save. I do this furtively, as if I'm stealing: slip the cheese slicer and nutcracker, the teeth and rattle and faded handkerchiefs into my bag, reminded of my fear of leaving pieces of myself—fingernail, tissue I've used—in a strange place. The way I whisper goodbye to my hair as I abandon it on a salon floor.

Let it go, my friend says, but it's not enough to keep the past in my head—I want the cardboard and cotton-ball Christmas wreath that brings it back.

◆

My mother still recognizes me, though my new iPhone doesn't. Three times I've set the facial recognition ID, circled my head to catch the angles. Each time I face it unrecognized, which confirms what I've suspected. I have no permanent face. I'm never sure what I'll find in a mirror.

My thumb's more reliable, more photogenic, my thumb pressing "home." But this new phone has no home.

I hate to say it, Donna, my mother says, but you look tired.

◆

A doll. Now that's a present.

◆

34

My mother can't remember the word for . . . what? *That stuff.* Snow? Trees? Curtains? It's too sad for words.

Yellow sweater, first zipper. Everything a souvenir of something lost.

◆

Without memory, this, here, a scrap of cardboard, a cotton ball.

Practice

We were told to put our heads on our desks, to conjure our sins and trespasses, examine them in our hearts. It was hard not to think about my lunchbox and would it be peanut butter again.

They led us, single file, through dusty halls to the church. I'd stolen chewing gum from the junk drawer, cut the bangs off my sister's doll. But we would recite only the opening and closing prayers, not our list of sins. This was our practice confession.

I was hoping for Father Donnelly, who was adored by our mothers and grandmothers and who'd sung *I Left My Heart in San Francisco* at the Communion Breakfast. But Father Murdoch met us in the church and disappeared into his box, instructing us to enter, one girl at a time.

In a few weeks he would be the first dead body I ever saw—pale and frowning in his wooden coffin. A wake, they said, as we lined up for the viewing. But he didn't look awake, lying on that velvet pillow. His vast nostrils, the sad rosary on his ruffled blanket.

One after another we entered the confessional, recited our prayers—*For these and all my sins I am heartily sorry*—and went back to our friends. The line got smaller. Father Murdoch opened his door and stepped out of the box. He whispered to Sister Agnes. The principal was called.

Some of us, it seemed, had not been heartily sorry at all. Some of us had confessed to being *hardly* sorry. I knew the difference. I didn't feel heartily sorry about my sister's doll, but I did feel bad.

The word was changed to *very*. I missed *heartily*. Now I could say I was very sorry about the doll, but the old word was still in me.

Heart attack, our mothers whispered. Had Father Murdoch missed that old word as much as I had?

But what if, I kept thinking, the girls who'd said *hardly* had felt, heartily, their utter unworthiness as they sat facing God and the screened, soon-to-be-dead profile of Father Murdoch? And what about the girls who said *very*, but thought heartily, and left the confessional forever suspicious of their own hearts?

In Cahoots

Our mother knew a lot of people in Cahoots.
We wanted to go there. *Look at us,*

my sister and I screeched, pulling
brown bags over our dull faces,

we're in Cahoots! Upside down
in our spoons, a collusion of roots,

we looked into the future—
which looked a lot like Cahoots.

The moon blued in our grim kitchen.
Oven mitts hung snug as a diphthong.

You could have a mind of windows in Cahoots,
Come Holy Ghost and multiple choice.

Paragraphs of blue in Cahoots. And singing
the old songs with our mother.

Follow the memorized streets
to the luncheonette, the red revolving stools:

here is a girl slurping her innocent egg cream.
Radio waves shake the unknowable

devotions inside her. May Day and snow day.
Rows of stubby pencils scribbling.

People died softly in Cahoots—together, on porches,
looking onto familiar streets, voices

pouring through them, holding their sister's hair.
Death was a comma. By yourself you were never

alone. Inside and outside, congruent as noon.

Kyoto 2

The sign in the window said:
you are here. And she was.
It surprised her.
It's not often she is
where she is, but she was
there, at the river, gulls
dipping, beating—
you're here you're here you're here.
She felt so proud to be there.
And then she wasn't.

Happy (*a zuihitsu*)

Sometimes I think I'm never as happy as I am reading a dictionary, gathering facts and etymologies in my notebook.

I'm an upbeat person when I'm traveling: in Monastiraki Square I am so happy to meet you! I love to sing! A chipper present-tense tourist in the land and language of the birth of tragedy. Yes yes yes! I say, though in Greek it's *neh neh neh*, and how optimistic does that sound?

◆

Why are you caught in one idea of happiness, my mindfulness book asks. That one idea can be an obstacle to happiness.

Whatever makes you happy, my mother used to say, meaning I was making a terrible mistake.

◆

Happy, says the *OED*, means "lucky," "favored by fortune," and comes from *hap*, meaning "chance" or "luck." Happy means that what happens turns out well. The luck of the draw.

Slaphappy appeared in World War II. As did *punch drunk*, possibly linked to *happy hour*, something my friend Kim introduced me to one afternoon in Sedona, where yucca trees and red rock mesas create spiritual vortices supposed to promote happiness, and streets are lined with fortune tellers, tarot card stands.

Happiness is not a potato, Lucy Snowe says in a book I love, the ending of which is notoriously ambiguous. You have to be perverse to believe, given the grammar, this is a happy ending.

How many of my most beloved books have happy endings?

None.

The main hormones that contribute to happiness are dopamine, serotonin, endorphins, and oxytocin. When released they make you feel happy. But are you actually happy?

In high school, we read a poem called "Hap" in which the vengeful god laughs: thou suffering thing know thy sorrow is my ecstasy. Hap isn't happiness, our teacher, with his long fingers and sexy ponytail, explained. Look it up. My love affair with dictionaries had already begun, but he did start me rooting around in words.

Stoics say happiness lies in lowering your expectations. To appreciate small moments of delight. Like kitty laughter, which is well below our threshold of hearing. I like to imagine my cats laughing in their kitty litter.

Eudaimonia, often translated as happiness, refers to the good life. A life lived, Aristotle says, according to our deepest values, not only for ourselves but for our community. It's not so much a feeling as a state of being.

I've been keeping a *Eudaimonia* list in my notebook: simple things people do for one another, stepping out of themselves to make a small, good thing happen. A jogger on Sixth Avenue stops to hold the door for a woman's unwieldy stroller. The doctor picks up a patient's dinner tray, stacks it on the refuse cart. A boy in a striped t-shirt waves out of an iPad into the blue tank of lonely Japanese garden eels to help them remember humans.

Why do we feel (we all feel) this sweet sensation of joy?

Happiness. Every string leading someone out of a labyrinth, the way slime molds and mycelial networks find routes through cities, a quick way out of Ikea. Or depression.

◆

I love to picture words, their roots dangling, spreading out, dragging their histories and uses and language families. And the word *rhizomatic,* something I call my rice cooker.

◆

Imagine a machine, our host says, that can give you—let you *feel*—any experience you desire: standing at a Piero in Arezzo, singing *Caro nome* at the Met. Around the table we conjure our desires: bringing food to refugees, writing a poem, brokering a cease-fire, trekking in the Himalayas. You'd really believe you'd done these things, he says, refilling our wineglasses, and won't remember programming this machine. Would you choose to remain in this state forever? Would this constitute a happy life?

I'm six, at the kitchen table with my mother, digging the eyes out of a potato with the tip of a peeler. My potato is full of holes. How can a potato have eyes? Holy potato, I say, as if it's the funniest thing in the world. My mother laughing makes me happy. You have a hole in your head, she says when I forget something.

Thinking of Mr. Potato Head makes me happy but remembering that old peeler and how much my mother is forgetting makes me sad.

More happy love! More happy, happy love! says Keats, who, in his last letter to Fanny Brawne, wrote: "I wish you could invent some means to make me happy without you. I am glad there is such a thing as the grave. I wish I was either in your arms full of faith or that a Thunder bolt would strike me."

What did I find in happiness? Pines, ashes, spies, pens, pies—

Perhaps it's not quite the right word.

Love Poem

O to finger the extravagant latitudes!
Press into the thumb tabs notching
the speckled edges! To start with A,

that January of letters. I never opened it
without hope or hunger,
rainy afternoons by the fire escape,

tired of limitations, the vagaries
of crayons. My friend had her own
room, a shag rug, a globe.

Pretty, the globe, but hollow. Monotonous.
Spin spin spin—a cape was always and only
a cape. But I could travel Malaysia

to makeup without moving, look up
in the shiver of pages, the titillating, forbidden
words (did you expect me to say them?)

the way you'd look up your friend's plaid skirt—
origins, histories whirling in each entry.
I wouldn't have traded it for the world.

Beloved students, you say it makes you dizzy,
gives you a headache. This red, shredding,
four-and-a-half pounds of infinite possibility.

Open it.
Every entry is a world.
I give you my word.

What Does Catastrophe Mean

a boy asked as he turned over a card and looked
into my future. Disaster, I thought—but no,
disaster means "the stars against us,"
while catastrophe is just "a turning over."

Watching Two Mourning Doves Mate on My Fire Escape While Playing Frank Sinatra over the Phone for My Mother

is not something I imagined myself doing, say,
five months ago when I was still calling them pigeons,
walking around without a mask and gloves

were something I wore to keep warm, lost, or found,
mateless, at the top of my mother's closet and tossed,
after my father died, after the three-hour bus ride

to Leisure Park, NJ, reading *The Empire of Cotton*—
I had to do something to keep from sobbing, remembering
the terrible video I took (how could I?), my father

tied to his hospital bed, rotating like a rotisserie chicken,
graph lines falling, rising, indecipherable. Cotton everywhere
I looked. Sheets, cheap t-shirts. Every cloud looked like cotton,

cotton threading every dollar. *Sea Island, American Upland.*
I've forgotten which was easier to seed, pick by hand, prized for
whiteness. Women were so identified with cotton they were buried

with their spinning tools. It was the seed that changed everything.
All spring, trapped in my apartment, I "had" two cardinals.
I learned to identify them—and white-throated sparrows, robins, jays—

first by look and then by song. I bought seeds, hung them
in a plastic bowl. The pigeons descended like vengeance,
swooped, swung, their dark capes clutching, industrious,

swinging, pecking, until every seed was gone. And the cardinals?
Never saw them again, though I searched with my father's binoculars,
peering into the unlikely apricot tree below. (Apricots! In Manhattan!)

Is it too late to learn about birds? And cotton? The three kinds of tears—
one type "viscous," I remember, as I listen to my mother's mind
slipping its history. Why learn again what you've forgotten,

will forget, lose? This line of thinking leads to . . . what?
The receiver leans against my speaker. My mother
is singing with Frank, her once-beautiful voice

remembering every word: *Love and Marriage.*
Fly Me to the Moon. The one fact I knew about birds—
they mate for life—turns out not to be true. The doves

are fluffing and preening. They mount briefly.
Frank is reaching the peak of another song.
Two years since my father rotated into . . . what?

Why didn't I learn to drive? Why didn't I learn about birds?
Have I imagined I was wearing innocent cotton all my life?
The mourning doves have flown, their moans

threading the trees, and my mother, glove
without a mate, sheet without a bed, singing
through the fibers, *That's Life.*

Real Simple

A place for everything and everything
so pretty! Whatever condition
you find yourself in, however untidy
the closet, here's a solution. Order
for any drawer, container for any fruit
or feeling. No more dead vegetables!
Leftover memories? Glass jars let you
see what's inside. Stacked by size
they keep and keep.
I bought a subscription for my mother.
When she wakes at night, crying for my father,
sweating her sheets with grief, she turns
a few pages, thumbs the hints and fixes,
the leftovers in their pretty coffins. Night after
night she reads herself to sleep. I am her daughter,
awake in bed with grammar books,
studying the conditional:
If you die you are dead
If you die you will be dead
If you died you would be dead
If you had died you would have been dead
If you hadn't been afraid to die you would have lifted your face.

3

Go Bag

By the time I notice the rifle range, the man in camouflage, the words—
hunker, grab, evacuate—in the instructional video, I'm already
deep in the woods. Like an overgrown boy scout right-wing survivalist

the man unboxes the Midland Emergency Crank Radio I bought but have
no idea how to use. With my candles & matches, pens, masks, flashlights,
extra meds & FEMA checklist, the Advil Tylenol Allegra, glue socks

batteries raincoat; with my ex-husband's bungee cord & fake Swiss Army
Knife (emergency corkscrew), a vacuum-packed jacket flat as a napkin
in its baggie, I'm ready. You wouldn't think of paper and pen,

Camouflage Man says. But it's the first thing I added, after the Band-Aids
& Bacitracin, the phone chargers, laptop chargers, charging stations &
rechargeable batteries. Why am I stumbling in the woods, no clue

to a way out? "Clue" from a root meaning thread or yarn. I packed both.
And string, which he says we can use to start a fire. I packed and repacked
as if I could plan my own disaster. Whistle in hand, equipped for tornado

fire flood earthquake civil emergency or attack. Isn't it a little exciting?
Stocking up, being prepared. Won't everyone be happy I brought string?
What had happened to put me in these woods? I've read Revelations.

Most of it. Twelve pages of catastrophe: boiling suns, bloody moons,
stars exploding in small print on that thin biblical paper.
It all boils down to pretty bad.

My cat is chewing a tuna treat she yanked from the pack.
Camouflage Man turns the Dynamo Crank, the LED flashes, the FM
blasting some awful rock I danced to in the '70s. I'm not feeling any

safer. Survival is improvisational. Luck. Chance. A game. This is X
but it could be Y. How many uses for a bungee? Yes, and . . . ?
Where is safe? Books are safe. And paper. I'm nowhere as safe

as I am on paper, holding the pen, edging myself west across the page
over to Sixth and Bedford where Marie has unlocked her car and waits
with cannisters of rice and Kind Bars, reading glasses, whistles dangling

from keychains we grabbed in a previous paragraph, radio blasting,
the car inching uptown through the ungrammatical run-on sentence
to Victoria—who will surely know where to go.

The Calling

She's been watching *Call the Midwife* on Netflix. One episode a night. It calms her. She thinks she would like to have been a midwife. To live quietly among women. Maybe she should have been a nun. Compline. Matins. Rising before dawn. Cradling babies. Though the idea of childbirth has always been a bit disturbing. Disgusting if you want to know the truth.

She hasn't had children, a fact of searing regret. Was that just one of those fixed ideas that had determined her life? Like driving. Surely driving can't be as dangerous as she makes it out to be. She has too vivid an imagination, her mother says. But how *not* to imagine her car swerving into a cluster of children. A baby stuck inside her because she wouldn't, she couldn't—my God, the pain! And they *would* keep saying *Push. There you go. Now breathe. Now little pushes.* She can see herself *saying* these things, watching the head, hours later, emerge. How many heads she's seen these three seasons, then the baby slides out—*slips* out, like a fish, the awful placenta trailing its cord.

Maybe it's Sister Julienne she's truly devoted to. Her infinite patience and quiet regrets. Her steady intelligent eyes. Opening her Julian of Norwich. A life of singing and service. Imagine not having to write the songs yourself or worry who would like them. Were they good? Would anyone sing them? What mattered was action, forgiveness, love.

Of course, the London slums are terrible. Poverty. Thalidomide. No birth control. Even the good policeman, the nuns, are homophobic (not Sister Julienne!). They hate the Irish, the Caribbeans. But they could change that, she and Sister Julienne, riding their bicycles through noisy streets in which the terrible is always balanced by the good. So soothing to watch before bed. A quiet world. An hour long. To live in a community, packing home kits and bottles of milk of magnesia. Comforting one another with cups of tea. (She's not a big tea drinker, but the tea things, the cups and cozies, *are* consoling.)

She misses Jenny, the principal midwife. Jenny left after a few seasons to play an awful character in *Wolf Hall*. Not even a big part. Now it's just Sister Julienne she's truly committed to, played by Jenny Agutter, who, she learned, leaves the show in Season 8 to be in a movie with Bill Nighy. Which changes things. She loves Bill Nighy. But this changes things.

"Last year I worked at this coffee shop, it was a warm spring evening and the place was empty, my manager was out. I opened all the windows and blasted this on the speakers. Music was flowing down the streets, people living in the nearby buildings opening their windows and letting music in. People were drawn into the coffee shop, they were so happy. It was the most perfect, divine moment of my life."

—YouTube comment on "Yimeji's Theme" from *In the Mood for Love*

—

I've been thinking about chronophobia, the fear of time passing. People with chronophobia can feel detached from their bodies and experience time speeding up or slowing down at random. Like calendar pages in old movies. Torn off days blown about by the wind: *February 23. October 24. June 6.*

—

Last night I watched a woman on YouTube explain 1000 years of Ukraine-Russia history in 9½ minutes.

—

Someone Googled: How can I see my true image?

One suggestion is to hold two mirrors together, just touching, creating a right angle between them, as if you're reading a book. With a little adjustment, you can get a complete reflection of how others see you.

Windows

I was thinking about Deep Time and small
windows of possibility, while, in the Arctic,

ancient methane was leaking through windows
opened by melting permafrost, and anthrax spores

seeped out of reindeer corpses buried in what
had once been frozen soil, then the swish

of windshield wipers, and I'm eight
in a neighbor's car, the turn signal ticking, the storm

beating the windows, and, for a little while, safe
in the backseat of the one who's not my mother.

Notebook

I list each morning sunrise sunset moonrise moonset,
every shriek and clothesline squeak of jay, each mournful
dove coo, panicked *chit*, as if I could staple myself to the day.
Yesterday was 2 minutes and 42 seconds longer than
the day before. My God, what have I done with my minutes?
Last night in my dream my family stood together,
all of us in a line, as if for a portrait. Or firing squad.
All our dead were with us. But "us" was dead.
Too vivid now my friend in his bed, out of reach,
out of power. Now the first full moon without him.
Lonely moon. Wolf moon. Only 99.8% full
but full enough. Soon we'll change the clocks.
What we used to do by hand now done without us.
Time changes before we wake. It's later than we think.
This morning I console myself by noting the three
kinds of twilight. The Blue Hour, the Golden Hour,
my cat, Lucca, resting her two-toned paw on my page.

for Richard McCann, in memoriam

Learning about Ants

I. ANTS

It was a twitch of busyness
stitching the concrete,

an itch of activity
without any discernible purpose.

They'd get in our slippers!
My grandmother in her flowered housedress

tossed her bucket of destruction,
agent of cleanliness and murder.

I can't remember how long it took them
to die, if they tried to escape,

whether my grandmother waited
before she swept them off our walk,

and why she didn't Clorox the chipmunks
we watched by her kitchen window.

Little apostrophe, little speck of grit,
so small I hardly notice it.

You. Flat scribble on a marble table,
a stagger, struggle, a drunken wobble

dragging something that looks like a leg
twitching, agitated, looking, well, *antsy.*

I hurt you, and shouldn't we have to watch
the suffering we've caused?

Do ants feel pain?
Can you say an ant looks dogged?

How helpless you are apart from your—
swarm? tribe? colony? your unstoppable

column, marching one by one and
two by two, with your high hopes,

out of the rain boom boom boom
spreading your terrible pheromones.

Now there's two of you. One of you
drags the other to the table edge

and the other drags you back.
Is this a dance? rescue? Is it sex?

I don't know yet about factions, colonies,
civil wars. How—vicious, unmerciful—

you capture one another.
Why can't I see you're fighting?

From different tribes?
You look the same.

3. LEARNING ABOUT ANTS

Now that I know the head, the thorax, the bifurcated abdomen,
now that I've labeled the jointed legs, the hard exoskeleton,

similar to human fingernails, now that I see the elbow-shaped antennae,
how the jaws evolve, the large mandible, the compound eyes,

small and close—numerous lenses stitched together (think soccer ball)—
now that I've learned about their surprisingly poor eyesight, the claws,

the small scar left after the queen sheds her wings, the stinger
that weakens the victim, the soldiers who carry it back to the nest,

the way army ants police across species—attack, bite, eviscerate, tear
limb from limb, abdomen from thorax, their sister workers, drag them

back to the queen to curry favor—now that I've watched the drama
enacted on this marble table, it seems to me they are as cruel

to one another as my grandmother was with her bucket of bleach.

Polyphony USA

They ran   hid under desks   in closets   quiet as shadows

                        now they would be a red dot on a map

   shoe in a schoolyard   a footprint
                        people will light candles   leave flowers
agitated flames dotting the night
                        they'd been singing
                                    row row row your boat
      zipping a jacket   just been to Target
                                    boy had too many freckles
white roof rising in his mind
                        gas station   movie theater   light rail   church

red dots spreading like measles
                                    Sandy Hook   Atlanta   San Jose
safe enough for a mother to
                        here's the stroller   a sandal
                                    it's happening again
   Parkland   Charleston   red dots bleeding
                                    igniting a mind
didn't like children
                        could smell them
                                    their itsy-bitsy spiders their row row row
My son Dylan
            four candles on the cake   one for luck

shadows in their plastic shrouds

kid upended a desk in fourth grade

we send money   fifty dollars

chalk lines   candles dotting the map

when I got to the station   it was like a movie

Las Vegas   Mother Emanuel AME

I'm ok but my friends are all

something about those drawings

pencil flames   eraser crumbs

sometimes in large spaces

I hear flowers in their plastic shrouds

Open the door   *Open* the door

It's happening again

We sleep the way you sleep after you've seen a scorpion under your bed

People will light shadows

again again again again again again again again

Psalm

*Thousands of dead and suffocating bunker fish washed up on the shores of the
Hudson, having succumbed to reduced levels of dissolved oxygen.*

Lord, we are junked on this forsaken shore—
 rocks, bottles, cigarette butts, broken concrete, all
  mountains of trash. We are trash. See us, listen,

for our travails are whispered by your waters. Blessed
 be the flies that flit and crawl across us,
  for thou hast been a shelter to our enemies.

We cast up our song to thee, Lord, let not our sisters
 suffocate in our home, we are sunk with our brothers,
  we are sinking and no one

to help us—not this woman who mourns at your shore—
 oh Buddy, oh Buddy—
  we are flailing in her shadow, her shadow

cannot save us, for thou hast made us
 bait over generations, our oils squeezed
  to feed the weak diseased hearts of men.

We keep steady the toxic algae,
 synthesize, release what green
  the sun releases. See us, Lord.

Our stunned eyes, mouths open
   as if death has surprised us.
      Hear us, have mercy.

Our time is vexed. We are driven, spin in suffocating
   circles . . . spare us, for blessed are we
      who, unsung, drown in our own house.

for Erika Fry

Windows

Each pane its own way of breaking.
So many ways for glass to shatter.
All night the breaking, smashing, now
morning crystals glitter in the gutter.
A brittle crazy glass, a heap of broken days
as glass, flesh as glass. Stripped mannequins
ripped from their displays. A leg, a wig,
an elegant French Revolution shoe. A foot
away, its silica packet no longer protects it.
So many ways for lives to shatter. A child
says what is the glass? Design Within Rage,
proclaims the cracked storefront window
where I'm looking back at myself, my face
in the glass making the outside *inside*
the way, when you slide your fist into a puppet,
it becomes, for the time being, a sleight-of-hand
dancing on a stage. Or a soul.

Are You Still Working on That

the waitress asked. I'm not working, the customer said. The waitress repeated the question. I'm not working, I'm eating, the customer said. Later that night the waitress, counting her tips, related this exchange to the others. One woman, a waiter said, when I asked was she done eating, looked at me as though I'd suggested she was a pig at the trough. I just say, *Are you finished?* But, said the waitress, when I ask that, people think I'm rushing them. Same with *Are you done with that? Can I take that?* not to mention *Can I wrap that up for you?* added another. The busboy, who'd been waiting for his 10%, explained how, tired of people demanding he *Take this away, please*, pretends he doesn't speak English. They all agreed there's no way to keep every customer happy. Although thinking about it, the bartender said, filling the ice wells, to ask were they still working bestowed a level of dignity on it. Camaraderie, said the line cook, a recovering addict, wiping down his station. Workers among workers, struggling together through this vast inscrutable universe.

4

Kyoto 3

Behind the road's low fence: goats—
brown tan white dappled, so
goat-like. They graze. Bells
tinkle in the light breeze. Two
kids rip leaves from the young
olive trees. Munch at the grass.
Shadows. The valley spreads
beyond and beyond that
mountains. Heat
so dense you could
weave a blanket out of it.
You should write about this,
a voice says. Bells in the breeze, it says.
And it's gone.

Webinar

There may come a time, the woman is saying

when you become incapacitated, she says

What should you think about before you become incapacitated?

Who would take care of you? Where would you want to live?

Rome, Audrey Hepburn says, looking at Gregory Peck, Rome is my favorite

Do your loved ones know your plans?

The questions hover in blue bubbles

Do your loved ones have time?

So much to do. Picking up broccoli, making Halloween costumes. Jacob's sushi suit. Ryan's red claw reaching out of the lobster pot

Have you considered whether you want to be . . .

Bubble to bubble: my future

Are you concerned about your beneficiary's spending habits? Who will inherit your . . .

All these books and no one wants them

Can I will someone my memories?

If I could have put you in a bubble, my mother said

Do your loved ones know your wishes? If you are no longer able to . . .

Let me stay in the past, window-shopping with my mother. Church Avenue. The Granada Theater. The matinee of cakes in Ebinger's bakery.

It's so hot, but it's the past, the heat, and I love it.

So much of my future was left in the past.

Today I wrote the word *always* and felt afraid. So much less of always now.

The Story of the Garden

I.

He's telling it again, my father,
the way he takes our neighbor in, shows him
the brilliant delphinium, hydrangea,

the hyacinths and violets, tulips and anemones.
Such abundance. Even the daisies wave. And the fruit!
Apples and peaches, the impeccable pears.

He'd labored for hours, twist-tying the plastic
lemons, oranges, nectarines, the artificial
blossoms and lush clusters, his Technicolor

trompe-l'oeil Eden, for the few delicious seconds
before our neighbor—he of the prize-winning
hybrids, the pretentious rhododendron—

understands the trick. Bruno, you son of a gun.
It was like pricking a balloon, the balloon seems
to enjoy it. All that work for seconds of pleasure.

My father loved to make people laugh,
but I like to imagine him lost in the making,
forcing our small dry yard into radiance.

I like to think he forgot our neighbor,
believing, in the intricacy of creation,
what beauty he'd made.

2.

The patient in the next bed laughs, listens
through the plastic curtains and linty blankets,
wheelchairs and IV poles, another room

filling with my father's marvelous garden.
I never saw it—the cinematic grapes popping
off their plastic stems. I'm tempted

to add birds, bees, ransacking imagination's
indiscriminate landfill where the smallest
artificial sprout shows there is really no death.

My father's garden heaped with doll heads, Barbies
bobbing among Tupperware lids and twist-ties,
never to degrade the way memory degrades.

But why pillage my father? A man
is not a diorama, an arrangement
of clauses and semicolons.

Here is my father. Here is his garden.
Bit of ink, string of sound, and here,
myself, my father's daughter.

The Figure a Poem Makes

It's a slow start. Notice the way
she's holding the pen. Four-beat line to open,
leaning blue, and—*synesthesia*—right at the jump.

If she can shift to the conditional—*yes!*
She lands clean on an accented syllable. Watch her
attempt this medial caesura. What a stanza!

What an effortless move across white space.
So difficult, the timing, writing this morning
to the radiator hissing. There's the phone.

She's been distracted before by the male
cardinal. *What a leap!* Her mother's thighs to—
oh my Lord—racial injustice. She's known for her

leaps, sometimes a bit reckless, but look at the way
she moves down the page. It's the years
of syllabics, all those sapphics—Holy

Smokes, what a line break! They don't call it
enjambment for nothing, folks. This has legs.
Notice her tight line, the way she recovers,

she's struggled with consistency, but, my God,
watch this right-branching sentence, a difficult
combination that was giving her trouble last year.

She is using this page as a trampoline. It's the
free-write of a lifetime. Oops, another wobbly metaphor.
Not her strong suit. OK, right here, rhythmic modulation:

Dactyls so tricky to pull off tonally, and
—smart move!—she substitutes a spondee. If she
slips up here, she can recover in revision. And she

nails it! Her friends are cheering. Her family
never noticed. Five years old caught her first feeling
in an image: birthday party, Pin the Tail on the Donkey.

Sixty years she's waited for this. The journals. The notebooks.
The shifting subjectivities. Now she's rounding the
turn, picking up speed—going for every degree of

difficulty here—she could falter (we've seen it before)
with one bad pun. If she lands this next element—*Yes!*
What a comeback after that disastrous haiku—Italy 2018.

She's gotta be thinking of her first coach,
Audre Lorde making her read Hopkins.
The years of loneliness, the losses. Her marriage.

To quote an abandoned draft: "Fuck the *Best of.*"
Gol-ly look at her. She just brought it in
on the biggest page in the world.

She doesn't need to wait for the score.
Sixty years to the day of Sylvia Plath's suicide.
What a story, folks. What a recovery!

Clams

The man has ordered Spaghetti with Clam Sauce. The woman is not fond of clams. In fact, she is not as fond of this man as she once was. The man begins to twirl the spaghetti around his fork, displacing several clams. He is frowning. She thinks of the expression "happy as a clam." How happy could a clam be? She tries to imagine what a clam might look like, happily swimming around the ocean with the other clams, but she can't picture this. They'd need fins—or legs—to even crawl. Maybe they just bob around like chunks of carrot in a soup. How happy is that? She wishes she knew what clams looked like still alive in the ocean before they were dead on someone's spaghetti. So many things she's never thought to imagine. She would ask the man, but he gets annoyed when she asks things like that. Things she should just know. He is not a happy man. She'd like to ask the waiter, but the waiter isn't looking too cheery either. She looks into the tangle of spaghetti, the juicy castanets in their parsley confetti. A gathering of smiles looking positively chatty! Still, she'll Google it when she gets home. Clams swimming. She would like to know more about clams.

Regards

I've been meaning to sweep these dead flies from my floor. Why so many flies stumbling along the windowsill? This one rubbing its hands, looking a little drunk, a little buzzed. What I took for glee was actually death throes.

Goodbye, goodbye, I cried, in a squeaky fly voice, at dinner last night, whirling, buzzing, collapsing in a dramatic heap. The life of the party.

◆

Today I read "The Crisis of Imagination Regarding the Future." We're number numb. How to mourn an abstraction, stop believing in the dialectical happy ending. Would that make us happy?

Happiness, Virginia Woolf says, is a table, a chair, a book with a paper-knife stuck between the pages. Reading makes me happy. Even reading Virginia Woolf with her terrible end.

The English major's in decline. A 49% decline in plumbers to fix our sinks. My mother's memory—that too down the drain.

My sister wanted to be a plumber, like Josephine in the old Comet commercial. Josephine seemed jolly. Is that the same as happy?

Ten years my sister dead. How can an ending be happy?

◆

The average American produces 16 metric tons of CO_2 every year. Every one of us is responsible for destroying 50 square meters (I'm trying to picture this) of Arctic Sea ice which, it says here, alters the way the planet wobbles.

What I took for geography was more like eschatology.

Biological annihilation. Extinction. Never again the Spix's Macaw, never again my father through the small window in his hospital chair, when I look back from the taxi, waving goodbye.

It was the last time she'd see him, but she didn't know that then. What a terrible sentence.

Start saying goodbye now, my father used to say, we're leaving in an hour. My mother took forever—*Regards, Regards*, she'd cry, kissing, hugging. *Regards.* The Italian goodbye.

In Italy to say goodbye you pull your hand toward you, which looks like *stay, come here.* Here you face your hand away, waving them off, until whoever it is has vanished, like the slowly disappearing dot in the old TV signal sign-off, which had always seemed like the end of the world.

I was adamant my mother would not die in this book. Adamant.

—

"When the head is cut off, the flatworm retains its memory, which resides perhaps in another part of the body . . . A strategy of groping."

—

I Googled "which bird sounds like a squeaky clothesline?" Seems a lot of people hear a squeaky clothesline when a blue jay passes.

—

I still keep her weather page on my laptop. Toms River. 49° there now where she no longer is.

Errands

I tried to ignore her, pleading old woman leaning on a tree guard
holding out a plate. I had no cash. It was hot. Late. So much to do.

Laundry, library, pharmacy, pet shop. I was lonely and limping,
my bags were tangled, and my friend had just died.

It was a sparrow—struggling, dust-brown, size-of-a-baby's-hand
shudder of feather stuck to a glue trap.

Please, she said, help me. She was shielding the bird
the way you hold your hand around a lit candle. Never touch a bird,

I learned as a girl. I dropped the bags. I touched the bird,
the beating chest feathers, tried to peel the trap from its twiggy

leg, slowly, the way you ease a Band-Aid off. The bird—I barely saw it—
shot up, swooped up, up into the tree, onto the fire escape,

the pet store sign swinging above us, then—gone!
A residue of feather stuck to the trap. We saved her,

the woman said. She touched my arm. I'm almost blind, she said.
She must have heard the bird, felt for the sound under the parked car.

How long had she knelt there, waiting, between the tree guard
and parked car, how had she felt for it among the cigarette butts

and gutter trash? How had she heard it above the racket of traffic?
Honeycrisps and Pink Ladies had rolled out of my grocery bag

and lay, shining, on the late sidewalk. Days I'd been waiting for a sign—
which might be why I thought of Jon. How busy the dead must be

at the beginning of being dead. So much to do. Even after you die.
So much we need you to do.

for Jon Tweedy, in memoriam

I Heard a Siren When I Died

and hammers, ladders, some bird's
provocative doppler, squeaky spondee

cheer cheer, car alarm and
who just dropped their garbage in the hall?
Beautiful recycling jostle of bottles.

Framed by the three twilights
of morning and the final twilights of night,
I died. So, you see, it dawned on me:

I was not alone.
Sound surrounded me
as I slipped through the teacup's crack

leaving it all: birds, books, my sturdy mug—
factory-made, infinitely replaceable—
the clown-faced Black Hole photo, inescapable

as the grave, virtual particle pairs, annihilating twins,
knees of homicidal cops. What a symmetry—
every morning the mourning dove dove

off its ledge. Every morning I tried to ask myself
a necessary question: who would I be without my memory?
What does infinity sound like?

I was born inside the whining sirens of Brooklyn,
red glare wheeling across our walls—and died
in a siren miles away. Fire escape to fire escape.

So much going on without me. Am I dead yet?
Is this heaven? Far back in language's big bang
heaven had the same root as chemise.

That heavenly veil draping a chaste sky.
Does the bird feel a twinge of fear before it
steps off? Is this memory of the fledge?

Church bells chime, endlessly symmetrical
echoes circle, cycle, sirens and
what is this music spooling out?

Telephone of the Wind

Meaning to point out the democracy of grief,
I tell my mother how,
after the tsunami, the grieving

traveled miles across Japan to an isolated
garden, an old-fashioned phone booth,
to dial up their dead.

Teenage sons. Widows. Inconsolable
daughters. "Sorry I called you stingy." "Our new
house is drafty." "Do you have a warm sweater?"

Untethered fragments, random questions
float across our call: Where is my car?
Who are these people? Out of the blue, we say

for the amniotic imagination. Where is the phone?
my mother wants to know. It's in your hand, Mom.
No, she says. The phone. *That* phone.

*

She Didn't Think It Was Possible

Lie back, he says, let your head go

back in the water . . .   a little more . . .

that's right . . .   breathe . . .   *good* . . .

see . . . you're floating . . .

now breathe out . . .   let yourself sink a little . . .

that's right . . . *breathe* . . .

I'm going to let go now . . .   open your eyes . . .

then the blue . . .   and the waves . . .

the waves holding her up . . .

Acknowledgments

Thank you to the following publications in which versions of these poems have appeared:

Academy of American Poets Poem-a-Day: "My Father Teaches Me to Play
　Solitaire"
American Poetry Review: "Go Bag"
The Eloquent Poem: "Postcard"
Five Points: "Diorama," "Beauty Parlor, 1970"
Italian Americana: "Ants," "Errands"
The Metropolitan Review: "To the Woman in Window 8 at the
　DMV," "Clams"
The New Yorker: "Midnight in the Pain Relief Aisle of CVS Thinking
　about *The Cloud of Unknowing*"
Poets for Harris: "Prayers"
The Providence Eye: "Are You Still Working on That?"
Women's Review of Books: "On Time," "Dust," "Learning About Ants"
The Yale Review, Poem of the Week: "*Real Simple*"

Impossible to say what my life would be without the crucial support and generosity, the inspiring work in the world of so many.

For your companionship, your invigorating attention, for every suggestion, thank you to my beloved writing group: to Marie Howe and Victoria Redel, for the many readings; to Nick Flynn, Sophie Cabot Black, Martin Moran, Ricky Ian Gordon, Vievee Francis, Mark Conway, Michael Klein, Pádraig Ó Tuama, and to Richard McCann (rest in peace, dearest). *What is now proved was once only imagined.*

Thank you, Catherine Barnett, for your steady, indefatigable encouragement, your rigor and insight and heart, and to Brenda Hillman for our ongoing conversation, your heartening, intuitive reading of these poems.

Thank you, Medrie MacPhee, my sister, and Kim Addonizio, *mia sorella*. Thank you, Sandro Stille, Daniel Mendelsohn, Stephen Simcock, Honor Moore, Kimiko Hahn, and Lynne Greenberg. My gratitude to David Masini, Judd Tully, Walter Mosley, Rachel Eliza Griffiths, Sara Rempe, Michael Thomas, Martha Rhodes, Karen Backus, Matthew Rottnek, Dimitri Mugianis, Tammy Chalala, and Tree Swenson. To Lili Taylor for the birds and Ghislaine Boulanger for all the years. *Grazie* to my Bogliasco pals: Kimi Takesue, Zuzanna Bulat-Silva, and Kurt Rohde. And to the employees at the Spring Street Trader Joe's.

Thank you, Roger and Sonia Celestin, for Syros and the sea.

Deep gratitude to Jill Bialosky for the catalyzing suggestions that sent me back into this book and helped to transform it. And to Julian Ansorge. who shepherded it through.

To Civitella Ranieri and the Bogliasco Foundation, *grazie, grazie, grazie*.

Notes

"Meditation": Quotes are from Walt Whitman, *Song of Myself*, with a nod to Wisława Szymborska, "Breughel's Two Monkeys."

"*Notebook*" (page 7): The quote is from Hirokazu Kore-eda's 1998 film, *After Life*.

"To the Woman in Window 8 at the DMV": See Montaigne's *Essays*.

"On Time": Notes on cadmium red are from Amy Sillman, "On Color" in *Faux Pas*. *Poetry* (2010) was directed by Lee Chang-Dong.

"Diorama": "The land of motionless childhood" is from Gaston Bachelard, *The Poetics of Space*.

"Beauty Parlor, 1970": In the 1960s Maidenform ran a series of such dream ads, which mostly appeared in "women's magazines."

"Kyoto 1": The epigraph was translated by Peter Constantine, Roger Celestin, and the author, and is used with their permission.

"Midnight in the Pain Relief Aisle of CVS Thinking about *The Cloud of Unknowing*": Quotes are from the fourteenth-century anonymous text *The Cloud of Unknowing* and St. John of the Cross, *The Dark Night of the Soul*.

"*Notebook*" (page 27): See "Crematory Is Booked? Japan Offers Corpse Hotels," *New York Times*, July 1, 2017; "Mushroom Suits, Biodegradable Urns and Death's Green Frontier," *New York Times*, April 22, 2016.

"Mouthguard to Kierkegaard": Misquote is from T. S. Eliot, *The Waste Land*.

"Happy": References to and quotes from Thich Nhat Hanh, *The Path of Emancipation*; the *OED*; Charlotte Brontë, *Villette*; Thomas Hardy, "Hap"; Keats's *Letters*; Elizabeth Bishop, "The Moose"; Samuel Beckett, *Waiting for Godot*.

"Love Poem": A dictionary is one of the most enduring gifts you can give a child. My first was the big red *Thorndike-Barnhart Junior Dictionary*.

"Watching Two Mourning Doves Mate on My Fire Escape While Playing Frank Sinatra over the Phone for My Mother": Facts about cotton are from Sven Beckert, *Empire of Cotton*.

"Windows" (page 58): For fascinating stories, gorgeous language, and sobering facts, see Robert Macfarlane, *Underland*.

"Polyphony USA": Contributions can be sent to *Sandy Hook Promise* et al.

"Psalm": Epigraph is from *The Journal News*, July 6, 2020.

"Windows" (page 67): Phrases (actual and distorted) are from T. S. Eliot, *The Waste Land*; Walt Whitman, *Song of Myself*; Psalm 103; Isaiah 40.

"The Story of the Garden": A nod to Walt Whitman, *Song of Myself*.

"The Figure a Poem Makes": The title is from Robert Frost's essay of the same name.

"Regards": See Bifo Berardi on the tyranny of the dialectical happy ending in *The Uprising: Poetry and Finance*. See also Virginia Woolf, *The Waves*.

Notebook (page 81): Facts about flatworms and fungi are from Merlin Sheldrake, *Entangled Life*.

"I Heard a Siren When I Died": Title thanks to Emily Dickinson, and the teacup crack to W. H. Auden, "As I Walked Out One Evening."

"Telephone of the Wind": After the initial news story, people were so taken by the idea that "wind phones" began to spring up worldwide. Now you can Google "Telephone of the Wind Near Me." Try to find the original Japanese documentary on YouTube.